Four Steps In Developing Your A.C.E.

Four Steps In Developing Your A.C.E.

Key Words to Success

"Attitude, Commitment and Enthusiasm"

By Cal Stevens
"Motivational Speaker, Musician, Photographer and Writer"

iUniverse, Inc.
New York Lincoln Shanghai

Four Steps In Developing Your A.C.E.
Key Words to Success

iUniverse, Inc.

For information address:
iUniverse, Inc.
2021 Pine Lake Road, Suite 100
Lincoln, NE 68512
www.iuniverse.com

ISBN: 0-595-33001-0

Printed in the United States of America

I am dedicating this book to my deceased parents: Emory Lee, Sr. and Sammie Edna Stevens. Without them and God, there would not have been this book for the world to read.

Cal Stevens

Contents

Foreword

In one important sense, Calvin Stevens does not do his work any justice. His writing's vital themes are no longer "nice to do" or "ways to improve." They are "must do," if the American economy is to survive as we know it, let alone thrive.

As an international consultant and a 13-year veteran of the speaking industry in the corporate world, I have been witness to enormous economic and cultural change in the past decade. Most importantly, I have seen the very personal impact of these changes on *people*. It has become clear to me that individuals can only perform their work well when they are fully committed to it. This is impossible unless the work environment effectively embraces change, as it affects *lives*, not simply business. Managers are learning that it is no longer practical or profitable for people to completely separate work from health and/or family. In fact, the most successful workers can be found in an environment that supports a balance of all three. This book was written for today's business professionals, to be understood in the context of both their work and personal lives.

Four Steps in Developing Your A.C.E. is designed to help you view and experience where you are today so that you may accomplish your wildest dreams tomorrow. Time and time again we've seen how successful people, no matter the color of their skin, succeed because they understand the principles that Calvin covers in this book. For those who pursue to understand their attitudes, stays committed for their journey and maintains their enthusiasm, are the ones who lead others who don't understand their personal A.C.E.

This book is written in a nontechnical and nonclinical manner for easy application by a wide span of employees, from CEO to the first-line manager. By focusing on the four key factors of A.C.E., a group, organization, or an individual can better the chances of maintaining true commitment instead of temporary lip service. No fluff, no babble, no fancy theories. Just down to earth "how to." This book works for business, government, not-for-profits, and volunteer organizations. In fact, it works for families, too, and for simply managing our own lives.

James Amps III
President
Amps International, LLC

Acknowledgements

I would like to thank God for giving me the insight to write this book. All things are possible with God. A special thanks to my wife of 36 years, Eleanor. Without her encouragement and editing, the final draft would still be on the computer. Thanks for pushing me. To James Amps III, motivational speaker from Florida, thanks for showing me that I could do this. A special thanks to Dr. Doris Sartor from Maxwell Air Force Base, Alabama, and Denise Spiller for editing the manuscript and offering positive suggestions. To my sister, Deena for your special skills in keeping me focused. To my immediate family of nine sisters and two brothers—thanks for your prayers. I would also like to extend a very special thanks to the Jones Family: Rev. L. J. and Tammie Jones (my in laws), Cheviene and Jean, Wallace and Fredonia, Theophia and Helen, Kenneth and Dorothy, plus a host of relatives, too many to name.

Finally, to my children, David, Calvin, Jr. and Tammie (a published author in her own right) and my grandchildren—Terry, Rosi, and Raven—what can I say? Love you all and thanks for being my inspiration. I sincerely appreciate the encouragement. To God be the glory!

Cal Stevens

Introduction

To understand me and where I am coming from, you will need to understand my background and upbringing. On March 30, 1947, I was born in a small segregated community, called Inkster, Michigan or "Cardboard City" just outside Detroit. It was called cardboard city because all of the houses were two-to-four family houses connected and made primarily of cardboard.

I was the sixth born of thirteen children of the late Emory Lee, Sr. and Sammie Edna Stevens, and raised in a household of nine sisters and two brothers. Back then, we never thought about the number of siblings, because everyone on our block came from a very large family. I never knew I was poor, because everyone in our neighborhood was poor. I learned to play the drums at 9. I played every day. While everyone else in the neighborhood was playing baseball and other sports, I was practicing on anything I could find to beat on. I did not get my first drum set until I went off and joined the U.S. Air Force Band. In any case, I learned two valuable lessons back then. Lesson one: practice did not make me perfect; practice made me practice harder. Because there were so many outstanding drummers in the Detroit metro area, you had to be outstanding in order to get any gigs. You also had to be able to play all types of music. Lesson two: I developed a positive mental attitude about what I wanted to do and where I wanted to go. All I thought about was music. I got so good, I began to play in the clubs in and around Detroit at 12. That, my friends, is a story in itself.

With 12 family members in our household, we had to have discipline. My mother was the disciplinarian. Because my father worked two full-time jobs to support the family, he was not always around to discipline me or any of my brothers or sisters. I cannot remember ever getting a "whipping" from my father. However, I can count the times my mother put the switch to my backside. I remember having to go outside and pull my own switch from a bush near the back door. Then, to make matters worse, I had to bring the switch to mother, so she could whip my behind! And don't even think of getting a small switch, because you would have to go right back out and get a larger switch. Talk about child punishment.

I grew up in a loving household. A fun household. A household where everyone was expected to respect one another, and to love one another. Now, back then, I could not understand how any one could possibly love a sister or in my case, sisters…who were always trying to tell me what to do. Anyway, those were wonderful times I will always remember.

Today, my two brothers (Emory, Jr. and Michael) and nine sisters (Legirtha Knight, Geraldine "Deena" Houston, Cordie Mae Kahr, Michaela Hall (Michael's twin), Deborah Archer, Jocelyn Renee Glaze, Carmen Latanya Reeves, Valerie Denise Stevens, and Kathy Lynette Stevens) are "still" living! In 1946, the Stevens family suffered its first loss. My brother, Wallace, having lived for one year; died in January of 1946 and the next year, I was born.

My parents always taught us to live life to the fullest and do our best no matter what others say or do. They encouraged us all not to hang out with the wrong crowd and to take the road less traveled. Although my parents did not finish high school, they were very wise and had common sense. Sometimes, common sense was all I needed to succeed in life.

I was the first member of my family to graduate from college. It wasn't easy, but I stuck with it and after six years of study, I earned my Bachelor's of Science Degree in Management.

Another value I learned from my parents was this thing called "work" or "work ethics". I have always held a job, no matter what. I shined shoes, worked in a car wash, wrote articles for the local newspaper, sold ladies clothes, delivered newspapers, shoveled snow in the winter, raked leaves in the fall and cut grass in the summer. I always had a job! Even while attending college, I worked 8 to 10 hours a day at the Ford Motor Company.

Even today, I don't have a problem with working. Right now, I am a member of the U.S. Air Force Reserves, stationed at Dobbins Air Reserve Base, serving as First Sergeant for the 94th Civil Engineer Squadron. I have always had the desire to use my skills to my utmost in order to be the very best person I could possibly be. By being a member of the Reserves, I learned discipline and learned how to deal with people on all levels. I am more fortunate than most because I enjoy working. I get my energy being around people.

Anyway, that's the general background of where I am coming from and now, we shall begin to talk specifically about developing your Attitude, Commitment and Enthusiasm or A.C.E.

When you begin to read the various chapters, I would like for you to think about what you will be doing in the next five years. Continue to plan how to accomplish your life's work or purpose, and then develop an action plan to complete this process.

1

Attitude, Commitment and Enthusiasm (Overview)

Chapter One

Attitude, Commitment and Enthusiasm: Overview

Attitude, Commitment and Enthusiasm, (A.C.E.)—these three words can have a profound impact on you and help move your career in a positive direction. Taken together, they form the basis of how you deal with life or how life deals with you. They have been the cornerstones of my career and if you allow it to happen, they can be the cornerstone of how you successfully navigate the rest of your life.

No matter what you think about these words, *ATTITUDE, COMMITMENT* and *ENTHUSIASM*, they are key and can be the beginnings of strategies that help you build a foundation for success. People are not born with attitude, commitment or enthusiasm. They are developed from a combination of four essential ingredients:

PASSION
PATIENCE
PURPOSE
PRAYER

Many corporate and government leaders say one or more of these are always at the foundation of their strategies for success. For these three well-known words, Attitude, Commitment and Enthusiasm, often defined and re-defined (sometimes used in a spiritual context), will be used to form the basis of this book for enhancing and developing your own A.C.E. Throughout the book, I will be using a variety of scriptures to explain and clarify my message.

It is easier to look through the lens of collective experience than to try and re-invent greatness. In this book I want to share with you what I have learned from years of leadership, crystallize the insights of other leaders, and give you a doable action plan for attaining the power in your organization and igniting your career.

If you feel stalled at the three-quarter mark of the race despite doing all the right things...if you're tired of standing in line dutifully as you watch others leapfrog ahead…if you're ready to boost yourself past the resistance and jump-start the next phase of your career, then A.C.E. should be on your agenda!

A.C.E. has been tested time and time again, and this method works. This method can place you among the real decision-makers where you can assume a role in determining policy and have a say in organizational strategy. Above all, A.C.E. can assist you in enhancing your personal and professional development.

Are you ready? Let's get ourselves some Attitude, Commitment and Enthusiasm!

2

Attitude

('ati 'tood)

"Your attitude determines the seasons you enter."

Chapter Two

When I talk about developing your A.C.E., I am really talking about understanding Your "Passion, Patience, Purpose and Prayer".

There is a common belief that your attitude determines your altitude. If you truly believe this, then, you are one-third on your way to a successful career and rewarding life.

Merriam-Webster defines attitude as "A mental position with regard to a fact or state; a feeling or emotion toward a fact or state." Nevertheless, attitude is more than that. Your attitude determines the seasons you enter! That is the one saying I've heard many times in school or on my job or in life—that is the importance of understanding how our attitudes affect others. We need to be more receptive to how others look at us. Not just on the outside, but what our attitudes reveal inside us. A positive attitude often determines degrees of success in life. In other words, "Your Attitude determines your Altitude." Do you feel you need an attitude adjustment? If you can honestly say yes, then I hope you will be able to find the right tools in order for you to make some changes or corrections in the directions you wish to proceed.

Dale Carnegie, profound author of the popular book, *"How to Win Friends and Influence People,"* wrote "Any fact facing us is not as important as our attitude toward it, for that determines our success or failure."

I agree with Mr. Carnegie. Often, our attitude usually stands in the way of many opportunities, whether on the job or at home. Sometimes, we miss our blessing because of a poor attitude.

Matthew 12:34, 36 and 37 addresses this issue: "For out of the abundance of the heart the mouth speaks. But I say to you that for every idle word men may speak, they will give account of it in the Day of Judgment. For by your words you will be justified, and by your words you will be condemned."

In this particular verse, the words spoken often reflect what is in your heart and can play an important part in the development of a positive attitude toward life. You recognize a person's attitude when he or she speaks. It's the tone of voice, the condescending remarks. You've heard it before. It's all reflected in one's attitude. Sometime it is hard to explain, but do you get the idea?

See if you can relate to the following words that make up your own attitude:

Opinion
Mental set
Experience
Point of View
Mindset
Disposition
Perspective
Choice

Many of these characteristics of attitude were developed in brainstorming sessions over many years, and they have become the choice of leaders. The opinions expressed in these characteristics form the basis of developing a positive mental mindset about life. In addition, there are the many years of experience, in our formative years, which in turn, help develop our individual point of view and establish our values and mindset about life in general. Together, these ideals lead one to implement a positive disposition according to one's perspective and finally, recommend a choice to which conforms to our own attitude.

However, attitude in its broadest sense is patience, purpose and prayer! Or, is it? Perhaps, the business executive has no patience what-so-ever; or the busy secretary who wants to find her purpose? Or, the manager who has never prayed? How do you go about developing or enhancing attitude without patience, purpose or prayer? I will go into further explanation of the Four P's in future chapters.

In defining attitude, we find these words—"disposition, one's feelings or mood toward people or things."

Which one of the above characteristics has a special meaning to you as you go about your daily life? One word that really stands out more than others to me is "choice."

Why choice? Because, in everything we do we have a choice. We have a choice if we are to be happy or sad. If we choose the right attitude, we can determine how we feel. It is our attitude that determines whether the road is paved with gold...or despair. Choices, good or bad, are left up to us.

The word *choice* or *choices* can also be reflected in our mindset. I choose to be happy today, no matter what. I will look upon this day as the best day of my life! Nobody is going to cause me to have a bad day! To improve one's attitude, you have to decide what type of day you will have. Again, choices! That's right, the moment you wake up in the morning, you and only you can decide if you are going to have a great day or an average day! You will have to make that decision. Will I have a great day? Will you? Will I have a terrible day? Will you?

Keith Harrell, author of the book, *"Attitude Is Everything"*, further defines attitude: "Your attitude dictates whether you are living life or life is living you. Attitudes determine whether you are on the way or in the way."

Here are a few "Positive Thinking" affirmations that may help you in determining your attitude. They are presented here now, so you can begin to use them daily and when you develop your action plan:

- I am Blessed and Highly Favored

- I am thankful for everything, especially my health, family and JOB

- I will not get so agitated at little annoyances—how important are they anyway?

- I will keep focused on my career and life—with more meaning than ever before.

- I will be more patient with co-workers, supervisors (yes, supervisors).

- I will take the initiative to do things to improve operations and services on my job.

- I will work toward getting more recognition for good works.

Positive affirmations are developed when starting your own action plan. What is an affirmation? An affirmation is a positive statement that something is so. Affirmations are most effective when kept simple, short and have an emotional impact. Wordy, complicated affirmations are to be avoided. Here are a few good examples: My worth as a human being is unconditional, and other people unconditionally like me; I am fully competent and capable in everything that I do and say; I am extremely successful in everything I do and say; I am a self-determined person, and I allow others the same right; and finally, There really is no one else like me in the entire world. I am unique.

Attitude determines the seasons you enter! Now, if you choose not to develop those characteristics that is YOUR choice! Remember, we are talking about developing our A.C.E., and these techniques will assist you.

The terrorist attacks on the United States on September 11, 2001, caused a tremendous change in some attitudes. Suddenly, minor things were not so important to many of us. As a result, our attitudes changed to more important circumstances, like spending more time with family or going on that much-needed vacation. In other words, these life-changing events resulted in new ways for all of us to measure personal success, happiness and opportunity.

Two events changed my life. The first life-changing event was the death of my father. Emory Lee Stevens, Sr., was killed in an automobile accident on March 1, 1984. I will never forget the long-distance telephone call from my sister, Deborah. "Calvin, I have some bad news. Daddy was involved in an automobile accident and it is really bad. They took him to the hospital." About an hour later, my sister called back to tell me Daddy had died! My father was the person who never got sick. He never complained about his aches and pains. He never liked to visit the doctor. I don't think he suffered, and for that, I am grateful. At that moment, my life suddenly changed. For so many years, my father and I were very close. I use to go with my father when he cleaned or "simonized" cars.

You see, my father already had two jobs, one at the Budd Wheel Company and the other at Sears. In his spare time, he operated his own sideline business, cleaning cars—what he often called, "simonizing." He had a special method of bringing out the shine in any type of car. Old or new, it didn't matter to my father. When he finished simonizing your car, you could indeed, see how good the car really looked. I had wonderful experiences with my father during my formative years. It was during that time, I learned the value of hard work and giving the customer what "they" wanted! I also learned my work ethic from him. My father got up "real" early and returned home very late. When he finally retired, he didn't know what to do with himself. I think about him often and all the good times we shared together.

The second life-changing event was the death of my mother, Sammie Edna Stevens, on October 2, 1994. My mother died of serious health complications. For years, my mother was afflicted with arthritis, and later confined to a wheelchair. In her final days, she was bedridden and unable to lift her arms or do anything for herself. She really suffered prior to her death. We all knew she would die, but one is never really prepared for the death of a loved one. One important lesson I learned from my mother was the ability to deal with pain. For years she experienced arthritis in her hands, they were very badly deformed. But she never complained. Deep down in our hearts, we all knew she suffered. She had a positive outlook on life in spite of her circumstances. She had that attitude you could feel. My parents changed my outlook in life. Everything I do is, first in appreciation to GOD for allowing me the opportunity to succeed in life and next, in honor of my parents. For they were always there when I needed them. I was more fortunate than most, because I grew up with both my parents during my formative years. That was a blessing in itself. For that, I am thankful.

My parents demonstrated the true meaning of having a positive attitude in spite of going through the challenges of life. They showed me and my brothers and sisters what it truly means to have a positive attitude and do not let bad choices prevent us from fulfilling the joys of living!

No matter what the circumstances, learning to handle life-altering events is imperative. Your "positive mental attitude" has a lot to do with the way you deal with stress of these events and how successfully you handle them. Learning to develop a positive attitude is choosing to be successful.

3

Commitment

(Ku'mitmunt)

*"Commitment is the decision to meet the needs of those
God has called you to serve"*

Chapter Three

As a musician, I played drums professionally with the United States 581st Air Force Band, Robins Air Force Base, Georgia. Music, as it is often said, is one of life's greatest pleasures and motivators. I can listen to gospel and smooth jazz all day and night.

Music is therapy! It's like CPR as it revives me and stirs my soul. The right music…at the right time…can be a healing balm. But sometimes music isn't enough.

Sometimes only four words keep me going just when I'm feeling overwhelmed with life. Those words are *Passion, Patience, Purpose* and *Prayer*. In spite of life's challenges, obstacles, frustrating days and unknown nights, I realized opportunities abound. Opportunities waiting for me…and waiting for you! But, only if you take hold of opportunities and run in the zeal for life even when you feel overwhelmed as I sometimes do.

There are even days when little things and obstacles seem to discourage me. There are moments when I wonder if I am going through a breakdown or a breakthrough. I find myself asking, "How long, when, who, why and how?" It is at these times I remember one word that was repeated by my first music teacher, Mr. Frank Harrington—"Commitment!" Time and time again, Mr. Harrington would ask me, "How committed are you in playing your drums? Do you want to be average or do you want to be great?" He would continue to encourage me so I would never give up. "Keep trying! Keep practicing! You are going to make your mother and father proud". I could not play football or basketball, because of my size. But I knew I could play the drums. Again, the drums became my motivator. I knew if I wanted to be better than the next drummer, I knew I had to practice harder.

There were times when I wanted to give up. My mother and father were my greatest audience. Sometimes when no one else in the family would come to hear me play in the band, I could always count on my mother. Because my father had to work two jobs, I knew he could not always attend my concerts. Nevertheless, he was proud of my accomplishments. My parents always encouraged me to do better. Sometimes I allowed my mistakes and the mistakes of other people or some other insignificant event or worry to deflate me like a pin piercing a balloon, but their encouragement, along with the commitment to be the world's greatest drummer pumped air back into my balloon giving me energy to RISE above my circumstances. Because of my love for playing the drums, I searched my heart and mind to find meaningful words to energize and renew my commitment in being the greatest drummer on earth!

Merriam-Webster defines commitment as "The act or process of committing. A pledge to do something; an agreement or pledge to do something in the future."

See if you can relate to the following words that make up your own commitment:

Focused
Performance
Zeal
Results
Belief
Persistance
Perservere
Determined
Purpose
Patience
Passion

Proverbs 16:3 reads, "Commit thy works unto the Lord, and thy thoughts shall be established."

I was definitely committed to learning everything there was about the rudiments of playing the drums. I stayed committed! Commitment at any level must be visible and sincere. Former American Express CEO, Harvey Golub says, "The values you choose are immaterial. Widespread acceptance and execution determine success." Being committed and doing the right thing becomes a habit. Commitment mixed with faith, confidence, determination and persistence cannot be denied.

Do you have your priorities straight? I asked God to grant me patience. God said, "No. Patience is a by-product of tribulations, it is granted, and it is earned." I asked God to give me happiness. God said, "No. I give you blessings. Happiness is up to you." I asked God to spare me pain. God said, "No. Suffering draws you apart from worldly cares and brings you closer to me." I asked God to make my spirit grow. God said, "No. You must grow on your own, but I will prune you to make you fruitful." I asked God for all things that I might enjoy life. God said, "No. I will give you life so that you may enjoy all things." I asked God to help me LOVE others, as much as God loves me.

God said…"Ahhhh, finally, you have the idea." Stop telling God how big your storm is. Instead, tell your storm how big your God is!

So, are you fully committed to life or is life committed to you? I ask you again, do you have your priorities straight? Others commit from a conviction that elevates personal values, which in turn, improve performance.

All of us must commit to something! Sometimes it is moving from old habits. Sometimes it is getting out of bad relationships. Many of us need to change our negative mindset. To be effective and fully committed, final actions require the power to leave things behind. Do you know what is holding you back and not allowing you to attain your promised future? Developing your A.C.E. helps you refine or design your action plan. You've taken the first step. Now, as you continue to read, you are making a commitment to life.

4

Enthusiasm

(En'thoozee'azum)

"The atmosphere you create determines the product you produce."

Chapter Four

Jewel Diamond Taylor, noted speaker and author, asks frequently during her presentations, "Are you 'On Fire' with your life? Do you look forward to each day? Do you have enthusiasm on your job, at school or home? What do you do that puts you into a zone?"

The zone Ms. Taylor is talking about is your "comfort zone". There are many books written about getting out of your comfort zone and learning to accept change. Accepting change for what it is. And for what it is not. James Amps III, motivator extraordinaire and author of the book, *"Speaking to Excel"*, talks about getting out of your "Zones of Comfort". For many people, change is hard. However, people resist change for several reasons:

- The current situation represents a significant investment in time, effort and money.

- Change represents additional work to some people.

- Internal change may indicate dissatisfaction for the way things are currently being managed.

- What is currently being done falls short of what *could* be done.

However, in order to maintain your enthusiasm and get out of your "Zones of Comfort", you must accept the following conditions:

- Include the people who will be affected by the change in the change process.

- Encourage as many people as possible to support the change. The more, the better.

- Know your area of expertise well.

- Be sensitive to the owner of the current condition.

- Do not blame your supervisors/managers, family/friends or spouse for your current condition(s).

- Encourage others to accept ownership of the change process.

- Encourage everyone to contribute suggestions and/or ideas.

- Indicate the benefits and rewards the change will produce.

- Approach your supervisor/manager with sensitivity and awareness for his or her investment in the current condition or situation.

- Be diplomatic.

- Remember—patience may be the best tactic. Your opportunity to influence change is not yet very far away.

Inspiring enthusiasm in people is hard. Noted motivator, Les Brown, often says, "If it's hard, then do it hard."

Jewel Diamond Taylor, James Amps and Les Brown have a zest for living. Enthusiasm is more than wealth. To become enthusiastic, you must act enthusiastic. When I played in the Air Force Band, there was a very talented trumpet player who reported for work every day, played his trumpet half-heartedly and was the first person to jump up after rehearsal and immediately leave the rehearsal hall. But there was the "less talented" player who reported in early every day and stayed late. He asked questions of the other trumpet players about certain musical phrases. He played with gusto, found it exciting and rewarding, learning to deal with new challenges. He displayed commit-ment to excellence and enthusiasm.

During my earlier days as percussionists with the Air Force Band, I poured myself into learning everything there was to be learned about playing the many different percussion instruments. I learned to read music. I learned to write and arrange musical scores. I was very enthusiastic about having the opportunity to be playing in the greatest band in the world! I was the first black drummer to play in the U.S. Air Force Bag Pipe Band.

Merriam-Webster defines enthusiasm as "Strong excitement of feeling; something inspiring zeal or fervor."

Enthusiasm is an expression of the dynamic vitality in your positive mental outlook on life. The way you walk. The way you talk. And, the way you act. "It is the positive result of your motivation and your physical magnetism and energy. It is the light in your eye, the timbre of your voice and the vigor in your handshake. Enthusiasm is power!" says Dr. Dennis Kimbro, author of the book, *"Think and Grow Rich: A Black Choice."*

In 1 Chronicles 16:31, we read "Let the heavens be glad, and let the earth rejoice: and let men say among the nations, The LORD reigneth."

Or in Psalm 30:11, "Thou hast turned for me my mourning into dancing." Continuing to Psalm 47:1—"O Clap your hands, all ye people; shout unto God with the voice of triumph."

"It is a quality that you must use as you march toward greatness." This is something we often take for granted. Being enthusiastic, but not taking the time to concentrate on developing an action plan or enhancing our outlook on life.

For example, Conrad Hilton in his best selling book, *"Be My Guest"*, says about enthusiasm: "It has been my experience that there is nothing worth doing that can be done without it. Ability you must have, but ability sparked with enthusiasm. Enthusiasm is an inexhaustible force, so mighty that you must never tame and temper it with wisdom. Use it and you will find yourself constantly moving forward to new forms of expression."

Once you have experienced enthusiasm or should I say, "cultivated" enthusiasm, you will be motivated by it even when times are tough. Though the chances slim and the odds long and everything seems totally against you, it is enthusiasm that will energize you and propel you to take action. The spirit of enthusiasm will allow you to go forward and lift you higher than you can imagine, especially during low times.

5

Four P's of Success

Chapter Five

Four "P's" of Success

Now that you have a clear understanding of A.C.E., let's take a look at the Four P's of Success. This is where you will develop an action plan for your A.C.E.

- Passion
- Patience
- Purpose
- Prayer

These are the four ingredients necessary to implement your action plan in order to overcome obstacles in your life. Most of all, and more importantly, they will help prepare you mentally to become the person God wants you to become.

These Four P's are four words so bound together, that success in one brings success in others. However, failure in one causes you to step back and think about your action plan and future.

These steps are necessary to enhance your professional and personal development. Each step will be defined and explained, but first let me ask you some important questions.

Are you committed to growth? The world is changing so rapidly, that the things we learned yesterday become obsolete seemingly overnight. Knowledge is the key to growth. You must love to learn and commit to personal and professional growth every day. Dr. Martin Luther King, Jr. stated, "I question and soul-search constantly to be as certain as I can that I am fulfilling the true meaning of my work, maintaining my sense of purpose."

Are you committed to action? To go to the next level, you must be able to identify specific areas for growth and then clearly give several solutions for action. The four P's will provide guidance and directions for responding to these two questions. However, only you can provide honest answers to fulfilling your goals and objectives.

Equivalent to a mathematical formula, success might look something like this:

A.C.E. + P4 = Success

Once applied combined with the action plan at the end of each section you will develop a sense of personal control and peace. One primary reason many individuals fail to achieve success is their inability to change or their opposition to change (re-read chapter four for the reasons why individuals resist change). Consciously adapting a positive attitude puts us well on our way to developing the mind-set to develop the five characteristics necessary for success.

Keep track of your progress by reading, then writing down your responses. Record the dates you have actually accomplished each successive trait.

After **twenty days,** you will have developed a strategy for personal and professional growth and ultimately, success. To be successful in life, you must first be willing to do something, take some action toward obtaining that goal. More importantly, you must actually take a risk in order to sustain that achievement. Are your ready for the challenge?

6

Passion

Passion ('pashum)

Chapter Six

Passion is made up of many words that describe how each one of us feel about our own attitude. Many of us have a passion in life. Perhaps, it is life itself! Perhaps not. Nevertheless, we never learned to develop a passion for anything.

I recall struggling with a certain drum rudiment, a fifteen-stroke roll, one of the most difficult of all drum rolls. Because of my passion in learning how to play the drums, I immediately overcame this obstacle. The burning passion and desire I had for playing the drums made me realize that playing the fifteen stroke roll was not that difficult after all.

Perhaps in your life, you have overcome obstacles. With an over-powering A.C.E., I am certain you, like me, can overcome whatever obstacles get in your way.

Below is an exercise you can use in developing passion for life. Do any of the characteristics describe you? Write down your answers here. Don't forget to include your responses in your action plan.

1. Do you show intense passion or emotion?

2. Do you have any objection of warm affection or devotion: "the theater was her first love" or "he likes football"?

3. Strong feelings or emotions?

4. An irrational but irresistible motive for a belief or action?

5. Something that is desired intensely: "his rage for fame destroyed him"?

All of these characteristics form the basic definition of passion. What must you do to gain the insight into your passion? Persons with passion recognize that the pursuit of excellence is the most powerful emotional motivator to succeed in life.

To understand passion, you will have to recognize your individual performance, its changes and its effects on your mental state. In addition, it is suggested that in order to improve your attitude, you may have to alter your behavior or negative attitudes. Once you are fully aware of this behavior and how it affects those around you, then you are ready to continue to improve other situations in terms of providing leadership with passion and respecting those you deal with regularly and those who are important in your life.

Merriam-Webster defines passion as, "The state of being acted upon; subjection to an external agent or influence; a passive condition; opposed to action. Capacity of being affected by external agents; susceptibility of impressions from external agents."

Macaulay writes, "The state of the mind when it is powerfully acted upon and influenced by something external to itself. The state of any particular faculty which, under such conditions, becomes extremely sensitive or uncontrollably excited; any emotion or sentiment (specifically, love or anger) in a state of abnormal or controlling activity; an extreme or inordinate desire; also, the capacity or susceptibility of being so affected; as, to be in a passion; the passions of love, hate, jealously, wrath, ambition, avarice, fear, etc.; a passion for war, or for drink; an orator should have passion as well as rhetorical skill."

I can tell you one thing about passion—once you get it and use it effectively, you will always appreciate having acquired an uncontrollable zest for your everyday life! Passion is the "stuff" life is made of! Grab it, hold it and finally, use it. In life, we sometimes think of passion as someone having love for another. Well, that's partly true, but passion runs deeper than that. Once you have developed your A.C.E., you are now on the first journey to establishing passion in all that you do.

7

Patience

Patience ('peyshuns)

Chapter Seven

Patience is the weapon forcing deception to reveal itself. Do you ever avoid what must be done because you are just not patient? How many opportunities and possibilities are never fulfilled because you were not patient enough when it was time for action?

In today's world, many of us live in a "McDonalds" world. In other words, we want it now! Can't wait, got to have it right now.

Merriam-Webster defines patience as "The capacity, habit, or fact of being patient."

In Psalm 37:7, we are told to "Rest in the LORD, and wait patiently for Him: fret not thyself because of him who prospereth in his way, because of the man who bringeth wicked devices to pass."

Whose patience is it anyway? It's yours and you have the option of adjusting your patience to serve your purposes. There are times when the best things in life will not wait until your patient mood happens to be right. There are times when it is in your best interest to put your patience aside for what must be done.

Here is a simple technique to use if you need help being more patient:

Let's say you have to complete a task; however you feel impatient about it. Visualize, clearly, richly and in full detail, how great it will feel to already have the job done.

The more you don't feel like doing or completing a task, the more you will want to have it done. Focus intensely on the benefits of having it done and that will put you in a mood to overcome your impatience and get it done.

Your feelings have a powerful influence on you. So focus them in a positive, productive direction and let them push you forward.

In Romans 5:3–5, we read "Any not only so, but we also glory in tribulations also: knowing that tribulation worketh patience; and patience, experience; and experience, hope. And hope maketh not ashamed: because the love of God is shed abroad in our hearts by the Holy Spirit which is given to us."

Finally, here are some encouraging words to help you overcome your less-than-patient attitude:

• Don't spend major time with minor people. Be patient anyway.

• If there are people in your life who continually disappoint you, break promises, stomp on your dreams, are too judgmental, have different values and don't have your back during difficult times…that is not a friend. Be patient anyway!

- Sometime in life as you grow, your friends will either grow or go. Be patient anyway!

- Surround yourself with people who reflect your values, goals, interests and lifestyle. Be patient anyway!

- When you think of successes, always be thankful to GOD. Be patient anyway!

- Over the years your phone book has changed because you changed for the better. Be patient anyway!

- At first you think you're going to be alone, but after a while new people show up in your life that make your life much sweeter and easier to endure. Be patient anyway!

- Remember what your elders used say: "Birds of a feather flock together." Be patient anyway!

- If you're an eagle, don't hang around chickens: Chickens can't fly! Be patient anyway!

- Walk by faith not by sight and be patient anyway!

"Knowing this, that the trying of your faith worketh patience. But let patience have *her* perfect work, that ye may be perfect and entire, wanting nothing."—James 1:3–4.

Knowing where and how to develop your strategy to overcome your impatience will carry you far in developing your A.C.E. You are now one-quarter on your way to success.

8

Purpose

Purpose ('purpus)

Chapter Eight

Many of us go through life; some even die before we clearly know our life purpose. What is your life purpose? "Having a purpose is the difference between making a living and making a life," says, Tom Thiss. In Ecclesiastes 3:1, we discover "To every *thing there is* a season, and a time to every purpose under the heaven." Notice I said, "life purpose and not purpose of life." If we live so we can watch how our lives unfold, and if we know what questions to ask our loved ones and ourselves, we will begin to understand why we are here. John 12:27 asks, "Now is any soul troubled; and what shall I say? Father, save me from this hour: But for this cause came I unto this hour." Rick Warren, author of the best-selling book, *"The Purpose-Driven Life"*, says it so eloquently: "Self-help books often suggest that you try to discover the meaning and purpose of your life by looking within yourself. That is the *wrong* place to start. You must begin with God, your Creator, and his reasons for creating you. You were made *by* God and *for* God, and until you understand that, life will never make sense." I totally agree with Rick Warren. For the purpose of clarification, our purpose reflects what we naturally DO best in life—the gifts, the talents and what our personality has to offer the world. How we aspire to BE in life—the qualities of our authenticity. In Proverbs 20:18, we are told "Every purpose is established by counsel: and with good advice make war."

Merriam-Webster defines purpose as, "Something set up as an object or end to be attained."

When I was growing up in Inkster, I truly thought my life's purpose was to play the drums. I was playing professionally in and around Detroit in nightclubs at 12. But first, I had to convince my mother this was my purpose. Of course, my mother, in her infinite wisdom, didn't buy it! Nevertheless, she reluctantly agreed to allow me to play in the nightclubs. Mobie was an organist and saxophonist who helped me convince my mother that he would be totally responsible for me while in the clubs. I played each set and during our breaks, I went backstage to wait for the next set to begin. Since I was so young, I was given a 15-minute drum solo to showcase my talents. The crowd loved it. Right then, I knew my life's purpose was playing the drums.

It wasn't until I started working for the U.S. General Services Administration in Atlanta that I really found my life's calling. I had the uncanny ability to speak before small and large audiences and there, I really found my life's purpose. After joining Toastmasters International, I set out to talk before as many audiences as possible. I spoke before church groups, civic organizations, any-where I could be heard by an audience.

God had a plan for me. And it was not playing the drums! Although I still play occasionally, I feel most comfortable speaking before small or large crowds.

When I joined the Air Force Reserves, I started out as a Carpenter Special-ist. Later, I was selected to become the First Sergeant, where the ability to communicate effectively was very important for success. I learned and con-tinue to learn how to communicate effectively, by listening to many great speakers. God led me to my purpose. Have you found your purpose? Often, we have a purpose in life.

God has granted us grace and mercy and we live our life's purpose in two ways: (1) By learning about ourselves and healing parts of us back to whole-ness, and (2) Through serving others in ways that align with our essentials of life. If you are having trouble finding your life's purpose, here is a poem that can get your life back on track:

A Creed to Live By
Author Unknown

Do not undermine your worth by comparing yourself with others. It is because we are different that each of us is special.

Do not set your goals by what other people deem important. Only you know what is best for you.

Do not take for granted the things closest to your heart. Cling to them as you would your life, for without them life is meaningless.

Do not let your life slip through your fingers by living in the past nor for the future. By living your life one day at a time, you live all the days of your life.

Do not give up when you still have something to give. Nothing is really over until the moment you stop trying. It is a fragile thread that binds us to each other. Do not be afraid to encounter risks. It is by taking chances that we learn how to be brave.

Do not shut love out of your life by saying it is impossible to find.

The quickest way to receive love is to give love; the fastest way to lose love is too hold it too tightly; in addition, the best way to keep love is to give it wings.

Do not dismiss your dreams. To be without dreams is to be without hope; to be without hope is to be without purpose.

Do not run through life so fast that you forget not only where you have been
but also where you are going.
Life is not a race, but a journey to be savored.
Be Yourself!

If that poem does not inspire you, then read Isaiah 14:27, which reads, "For
the LORD of hosts hath purposed, and who shall disannul it? And his hand is
stretched out, and who shall turn it back?"

9

Prayer

Prayer (Prehr)

Chapter Nine

The final "P", Prayer, is something we all need daily. However, life has a way of preventing us from praying in a way that is pleasing to God. Sometimes we get so wrapped in small and insignificant things, we fail or do not stop and thank God for life and His many blessings!

In 1934, Reinhold Niebur, composed a poem or prayer in Heath, MA, entitled the "Serenity Prayer". I know many of you have probably read this prayer. Over the years, this prayer has become the motto of Alcoholics Anonymous.

<u>Serenity Prayer</u>

God, grant me the serenity
to accept the things
I cannot change.
Courage to change the
things I can, and
the Wisdom to know the difference.
Living one day at a time;
Enjoying one moment at a time;
Accepting hardship as the
pathway to peace.
Taking, as He did, this
sinful world as it is,
not as I would have it.
Trusting that he will make
all things right if I
surrender to His will;
That I may be reasonably happy
in this life, and supremely
happy with Him forever in
the next. Amen.

Many people never realized there were other parts to this very popular prayer. So what does this all mean? It means no matter how talented we are, no matter how important we think we are, or no matter how little we think about ourselves, there is always a need for prayer. If you think you have accomplished all there is in life and have pulled yourself up by your bootstraps, then, you really need prayer! Where is your life headed? It may seem like it's headed nowhere. It may seem really confusing. It may not make much sense. Here's the beauty: wherever we are in life, whatever it is that we are doing, it is happening for a reason. Today we are creating our destiny, whether we realize it or not. Above all, prayer helps. Prayer changes things.

In I Thessalonians 5:17, we are told to "Pray without ceasing." Here are some strategies to assist you in your prayer development:

- Begin your prayer by praying for those closest to you. Pray for your loved ones. They are the easiest to remember.

- Pray for those who have mentored to you over the years.

- Pray for your enemies! Yes, pray for your enemies.

- Pray for those who teach, instruct and heal. Which includes, teachers, ministers and doctors. These individuals need support and wisdom in pointing others in the right direction. Always keep them in your prayers.

- Pray for our leaders. No matter what political persuasion.

- Pray for leaders in business and industry. For these individuals shape our nation and guide public opinion. They always need God's guidance.

- Pray for the weak, those in trouble or in pain. They need our prayers day and night. We cannot pray too much for them.

- Finally, pray for ourselves in relation to God and others.

In II Chronicles 7:14, we are promised, "If My people, which are called by My name, shall humble themselves, and pray and seek My face, and turn from their wicked ways, then will I hear from heaven, and will forgive their sin and will heal their land."

The last shall be first and the first shall be last. By the time you have prayed for the others, your own needs will have to be placed into proper perspective and you will be able to pray for yourself more effectively.

For those who don't have much time to pray or don't think they have time to pray—the busy single mother, the over-worked executive—those people who need to know they can pray to God anytime, anyplace in any location.

As I close on these four steps of success, I would like to leave you with this anonymous prayer:

Prayer Before Starting Work

My Heavenly Father, as I enter this work place, I bring
Your presence with me. I speak your peace, Your grace,
Your mercy, and Your perfect order into this office. I
Acknowledge Your power over all that will be spoken,
Thought, decided, and done within these walls.
Lord, I thank You for the gifts you have blessed me with.
I commit to using them responsibly in Your honor. Give
me a fresh supply of strength to do my job. Anoint my
projects, ideas, and energy; so that even my smallest
accomplishment may bring you glory.
Lord, when I am confused, guide me. When I am weary,
energize me. When I am burned out, infuse me with the
light of the Holy Spirit. May the work that I do and the
way I do it bring faith, joy, and a smile to all that I come
in contact with today. And oh Lord, when I leave this
place, give me mercy as I travel. Bless my family and
home to be in order as I left it. Lord, I thank you for
everything You've done, everything You're doing, and
everything You're going to do.
In the Name of Jesus I pray, with much love and Thanksgiving…Amen

Remember, thought determines what you *want*; action determines what you *get!*

10

My Action Plan

Instructions for completing your action plan

This action plan will assist you in refocusing your efforts towards success, after reviewing the concepts of A.C.E., you are now ready to build that lasting foundation:

1. Start with a date you wish to develop your four P's.

2. Continue to write in dates in the sixteen blocks as you develop your action plan.

3. Read the five characteristics or action steps to develop your thinking about your life's purpose.

4. Write down what you feel about each of the five characteristics in the blank spaces:

    —Possessing self-awareness
    —Managing emotions
    —Motivating oneself appropriately
    —Having empathy
    —Handling relationships

5. Concentrate on these characteristics you feel you are lacking and work to develop a clear path for improvement."Bite off more than you can chew, and then chew it. Plan more than you can do, and then do it!"—Anonymous

Action Plan in Developing Passion, Patience, Purpose and Prayer in My Daily Life:

Date Begin: _____ Date Ended: _____

(Note: Write in the date each time you practice the five action steps)

It is very important that you keep a daily log of your awareness and practice of the five action steps. Please read each of the five action step descriptions and write down what you think you should be working on to develop your four steps of success. If you need to go back and re-read the four chapters describing passion, patience, purpose and prayer, then take the time necessary to re-acquaint yourself with the definitions and other clarifications.

Action Step 1

Possessing self-awareness: Observing oneself and recognizing a feeling as it happens:

_____

Action Step 1 Continued

Action Step 2

Managing emotions: Handling feelings so they are appropriate. Realizing what is behind a feeling. Handling fears and anxieties, anger and sadness:

_____

Action Step 2 Continued

Action Step 3

Motivating oneself appropriately: Channeling emotions in the service of a goal. Practicing emotional self-control. Delaying gratification and stifling impulses:

Action Step 3 Continued

Action Step 4

Having empathy: Showing sensitivity to others' feelings and concerns. Taking their perspective and appreciating the differences in how people feel about things:

_____

Action Step 4 Continued

Action Step 5

Handling relationships: Managing emotions in others. Having social competence and social skills:

_____

Action Step 5 Continued

Congratulations on completing the final step in developing your Attitude, Commitment and Enthusiasm! Now, the rest is up to you. I hope you have gained an awareness of and an appreciation for your ability to improve your outlook in life and more importantly that you seek to find the real you. If you have faithfully developed an action plan, then you are well on your way to successfully navigating the rest of your life.

With passion, patience, purpose and prayer, you can control your own destiny and achieve mastery of your personal and professional life!

Motivational Reading List

"Attitude Is Everything, A Tune-Up to Enhance Your Life", Keith Harrell Kendall/Hunt Publishing Company, 1995.

"Attitude Is Everything", Keith Harrell, Harper Collins Publishing, Inc., 2000.

"Enlightened Leadership: Getting to the Heart of Change", Ed Oakley and Doug Krug, Simon and Schuster: Fireside, 1991.

"Think and Grow Rich: A Black Choice", Dr. Dennis Kimbro and Napoleon Hill, Ballantine Books, 1991.

"It Only Takes A Minute to Change Your Life", Willie Jolley, St. Martin's Press, 1997.

"The Greatest Salesman in the World", Og Mandino, Frederick Fell, Inc., 1968.

"The Seven Habits of Highly Effective People", Dr. Stephen R. Covey, First Fireside, 1989.

"Speaking to Excel", James Amps III, Amps Communications, 2000.

"How to Win Friends and Influence People", Dale Carnegie, Pocket Books, 1936, 1964 and 1981.

"Be My Guest", Conrad Hilton, A Fireside Book, 1957.

"In Pursuit of Purpose", Dr. Myles Munroe, Destiny Image Publishers, 1995.

"The Purpose-Driven Life", Rick Warren, Zondervan, 2002.

"The Power of Purpose: Creating Meaning in Your Life and Work", Richard J. Leider, Berrett-Koehler Publishers, 1997.

NOTE: This is not an exclusive list. You will need to establish a reading program that includes reading other motivational books.

"Four Steps in Developing Your Attitude, Commitment and Enthusiasm"

Four Easy Ways to Order:

FAX ORDERS: 404.288.3604
TELEPHONE ORDERS: 1.888.291.4995, Pin 9183 or 404.288.3604
EMAIL ORDERS: sales@tacadamarketing.com
POSTAL ORDERS: TACADA Marketing, P.O. Box 373855, Deca-
                                  tur, GA 30037-3855

Please send the following book: "Four Steps in Developing Your
A.C.E."—$11.95 plus $3.95 shipping (GA residents add 7.0% tax):

NAME: _____

ADDRESS: _____

CITY: _____

STATE: _____ ZIP: _____

TELEPHONE: _____

EMAIL (Optional): _____

Please send FREE information on: "Please Circle"
     Other books   Speaking/Seminars   Consulting

PAYMENT: _____   Check/Money Order   Credit Card: "Circle"

     VISA   MASTERCARD   AMERICAN
                                                            EXPRESS

CARD NUMBER: _____

NAME ON CARD: _____

EXPIRATION DATE: _____

"Four Steps in Developing Your Attitude, Commitment and Enthusiasm"

Four Easy Ways to Order:

FAX ORDERS: 404.288.3604
TELEPHONE ORDERS: 1.888.291.4995, Pin 9183 or 404.288.3604
EMAIL ORDERS: sales@tacadamarketing.com
POSTAL ORDERS: TACADA Marketing, P.O. Box 373855, Decatur, GA 30037-3855

Please send the following book: "Four Steps in Developing Your A.C.E."—$11.95 plus $3.95 shipping (GA residents add 7.0% tax):

NAME: _____

ADDRESS: _____

CITY: _____

STATE: _____ ZIP: _____

TELEPHONE: _____

EMAIL (Optional): _____

Please send FREE information on: "Please Circle"
Other books   Speaking/Seminars   Consulting

PAYMENT: _____ Check/Money Order   Credit Card: "Circle"

VISA   MASTERCARD   AMERICAN EXPRESS

CARD NUMBER: _____

NAME ON CARD: _____

EXPIRATION DATE: _____

"Four Steps in Developing Your Attitude, Commitment and Enthusiasm"

Four Easy Ways to Order:

FAX ORDERS: 404.288.3604
TELEPHONE ORDERS: 1.888.291.4995, Pin 9183 or 404.288.3604
EMAIL ORDERS: sales@tacadamarketing.com
POSTAL ORDERS: TACADA Marketing, P.O. Box 373855, Deca-
                                     tur, GA 30037-3855

Please send the following book: "Four Steps in Developing Your
A.C.E."—$11.95 plus $3.95 shipping (GA residents add 7.0% tax):

NAME: _____

ADDRESS: _____

CITY: _____

STATE: _____ ZIP: _____

TELEPHONE: _____

EMAIL (Optional): _____

Please send FREE information on: "Please Circle"
       Other books   Speaking/Seminars   Consulting

PAYMENT: _____   Check/Money Order   Credit Card: "Circle"

       VISA   MASTERCARD   AMERICAN
                                                                    EXPRESS

CARD NUMBER: _____

NAME ON CARD: _____

EXPIRATION DATE: _____

"A New Motivational Presentation"
By Cal Stevens

This powerful presentation speaks to greatness and challenges us to develop our own Attitude, Commitment and Enthusiasm.

Four Steps in Developing Your A.C.E. is for everyone who is seeking to control their own destiny and to achieve mastery of their personal and professional life.

For the last fifteen years, Cal Stevens has entertained and inspired audiences of all ages throughout the United States.

His presentations (as well as his professional development seminars and workshops) are energetic, spirited and fun filled.
Other noteworthy presentations:

"What Seeds Are You Sowing?"
"Developing A Whatever-It-Takes Attitude"
"Five Principles of Success"

FOR BOOKING INFORMATION:

Call, write or email to:

TACADA Marketing
2765 DaVinci Crescent
Decatur, GA 30034-3122

1.888.291.4995 ext 9183
404.288.3604

president@tacadamarketing.com

www.tacadamarketing.com

REMEMBER:

Thought determines

What you want,

Action determines

What you get!

CPSIA information can be obtained at www.ICGtesting.com
Printed in the USA
LVOW041450120911

245937LV00001B/33/A

9 780595 330010